MW00905665

To

From

On My Knees

*H*ow vital that we pray, armed with the knowledge that God is in heaven. Pray with any lesser conviction and your prayers are timid, shallow, and hollow. But spend some time walking in the workshop of the heavens, seeing what God has done, and watch how your prayers are energized.

MAX LUCADO

January 1

When we succeed in truly thanking God, we feel good at heart. The reason is that we have been created to give glory to God, now and forevermore. And every time we do so, we feel that we are in harmony with His plans and purpose for our lives. Then we are truly in our element. That is why it is so blessed.

O. HALLESBY

Giving thanks unto the Father.
COLOSSIANS 1:12

December 31

It is not so true that "prayer changes things" as that prayer changes me and I change things. God has so constituted things that prayer on the basis of Redemption alters the way in which a man looks at things. Prayer is not a question of altering things externally, but of working wonders in a man's disposition.

O. CHAMBERS

January 2

*J*esus Christ carries on intercession for us in heaven; the Holy Ghost carries on intercession in us on earth; and we the saints have to carry on intercession for all men.

O. CHAMBERS

December 30

The Spirit of prayer makes us so intimate with God that we scarcely pass through an experience before we speak to Him about it, either in supplication, in sighing, in pouring out our woes before Him, in fervent requests, or in thanksgiving and adoration.

O. HALLESBY

I am my beloved's, and his desire is toward me.

SONG OF SOLOMON 7:10

January 3

*H*e who is too busy to pray will be too busy to live a holy life. Satan had rather we let the grass grow on the path to our prayer chamber than anything else.

E. M. BOUNDS

December 29

)t is through Him, as our mediator, that we address God as our Father with our prayers and our sacrifices of praise. The gifts we ask for do not come then through our ears or our nostrils. They come from Him who is our mouth, our taste, our wisdom, so that there is nourishment to all who receive Him.

BERNARD OF CLAIRVAUX

January 4

*T*he work of praying is prerequisite to all other work in the kingdom of God. By prayer we couple the powers of heaven to our helplessness, the powers which can capture strongholds and make the impossible possible.

O. HALLESBY

With God all things are possible.
MATTHEW 19:26

December 28

Let us pray for the Spirit of prayer. He will take us into the workshop where the power conduits lie. Above the door of this room is written: "Nothing shall be impossible unto you."

O. HALLESBY

January 5

Lord Jesus, cause me to know in my daily experiences the glory and sweetness of Thy name, and then teach me how to use it in my prayers, so that I may be a prince prevailing with God.

C. H. SPURGEON

For as a prince hast thou power with God and with men, and hast prevailed.

GENESIS 32:28

December 27

*G*et into the habit of dealing with God about everything. Unless in the first waking moment of the day you learn to fling the door wide back and let God in, you will work on a wrong level all day; but swing the door wide open and pray to your Father in secret, and every public thing will be stamped with the presence of God.

O. CHAMBERS

January 6

*P*ray because you have a Father, not because it quietens you, and give Him time to answer.

O. CHAMBERS

December 26

*T*hat man is the most immortal who has done the most and the best praying. The man of many and acceptable prayers has done the truest and greatest service to the incoming generation.

E. M. BOUNDS

Wherefore lift up thy prayer.
2 KINGS 19:4

January 7

Fellowship with God in Jesus Christ will lead us to the experience that there is no good thing in us, and that we can have fellowship with God only as our faith becomes a humbling of ourselves as Christ humbled himself, and we truly live in Him as He is in the Father.

A. MURRAY

He humbled himself, and became obedient.
PHILIPPIANS 2:8

December 25

As white snowflakes fall quietly and thickly on a winter day, answers to prayer will settle down upon you at every step you take, even to your dying day. The story of your life will be the story of prayer and answers to prayer.

O. HALLESBY

Goodness and mercy shall follow me all the days of my life.

PSALM 23:6

January 8

God's cause is committed to men; God commits himself to men. Praying men are the vicegerents of God; they do His work and carry out His plans.

E. M. BOUNDS

Oh thou that hearest prayer,
unto thee shall all flesh come.

PSALM 65:2

December 24

Apostasy generally begins at the closet door. Be much in secret fellowship with God.

PHILIP HENRY

Pray to thy Father which is in secret.

MATTHEW 6:6

January 9

*B*egin to realize more and more that prayer is the most important thing you do. You can use your time to no better advantage than to pray whenever you have an opportunity to do so, either alone or with others, while at work, while at rest, or while walking down the street. Anywhere!

O. HALLESBY

December 23

*I*f I am a Christian, I am not set on saving my own skin, but on seeing that the salvation of God comes through me to others, and the great way is by intercession.

O. CHAMBERS

We give thanks to God always for you all, making mention of you in our prayers.

1 THESSALONIANS 1:2

January 10

Whenever the insistence is on the point that God answers prayer, we are off the track. The meaning of prayer is that we get hold of God, not of the answer.

O. CHAMBERS

December 22

*L*et it be your business every day, in the secrecy of the inner chamber, to meet the holy God. You will be repaid for the trouble it may cost you. The reward will be sure and rich.

A. MURRAY

He that is holy, let him be holy still.
REVELATION 22:11

January 11

*T*hink how in the inner chamber the hour of prayer may become the happiest time in the whole day for us, and how God may use us to take a share in the carrying out of His plans, and make us fountains of blessing for the world around us.

A. MURRAY

That they may see your good works,
and glorify your Father.
MATTHEW 5:16

December 21

Our faith in prayer can be no passing attitude that changes with the wind or with our own feelings and circumstances; it must be a fact that God hears and answers, that His ear is ever open to the cry of His children, and that the power to do what is asked of Him is commensurate with His willingness.

E. M. BOUNDS

We will give ourselves continually to prayer.

ACTS 6:4

J a n u a r y   1 2

The Spirit must be given an opportunity to reveal Christ to us every day. This is absolutely essential. Christ is such that we need only "see" Him, and prayer will rise from our hearts. Voluntary prayer, confident prayer.

O. HALLESBY

He shall glorify me: for he shall receive of mine, and shall shew it unto you.

JOHN 16:14

December 20

*I*n prayer the Church has received power to rule the world. The Church is always the little flock. But if it would stay together on its knees, it would dominate world politics—from the prayer room.

O. HALLESBY

All continued with one accord in prayer.
ACTS 1:14

J a n u a r y   1 3

The cause of God has one golden age, and that is the age of prayer. When its leaders are men of prayer, when prayer is the prevailing element of worship, like the incense giving continual fragrance to its service, then the cause of God will be triumphant.

E. M. BOUNDS

December 19

Intercessory prayer for one who is sinning prevails. God says so! The will of the man prayed for does not come into question at all, he is connected with God by prayer, and prayer on the basis of the Redemption sets the connection working and God gives life.

O. CHAMBERS

He bare the sin of many, and made intercession for the transgressors.

ISAIAH 53:12

January 14

*I*f we are abiding in Jesus and His words are abiding in us, then Jesus says God will answer our prayers.

O. CHAMBERS

Ye shall ask what ye will,
and it shall be done unto you.

JOHN 15:7

December 18

Tomorrow I plan to work, work, from early until late. In fact, I have so much to do that I shall spend the first three hours in prayer.

MARTIN LUTHER

*In the morning will I direct
my prayer unto thee.*

PSALM 5:3

JANUARY 15

Thy name is my passport, and secures me access;
Thy name is my plea, and secures me answer;
Thy name is my honor, and secures me glory.
Blessed Name, Thou art honey in my mouth,
music in my ear, heaven in my heart,
and all in all to all my being!

C. H. SPURGEON

How sweet are thy words…
sweeter than honey to my mouth!
PSALM 119:103

December 17

*G*od, at times, even grants the prayers of the unconverted for the same reason that He showers other blessings upon them, namely, because He loves them and desires to save them. Answer to prayer becomes one of the gracious means whereby God seeks to bring such people to repentance.

O. HALLESBY

January 16

The prayer chamber conserves our relation to God. Then Satan has to break our hold on, and close up our way to the prayer chambers, ere he can break our hold on God or close up our way to heaven.

E. M. BOUNDS

December 16

*I*t is only when the whole heart is gripped with the passion of prayer that the life-giving fire descends, for none but the earnest man gets access to the ear of God.

E. M. BOUNDS

Ye shall...find me, when ye shall search for me with all your heart.

JEREMIAH 29:13

January 17

*G*od alone fully understands what each one
of us needs; we make mistakes continually
and pray for things which would be harmful
to us if we received them. Afterwards we see
our mistakes and realize that God is good
and wise in not giving us these things, even
though we plead ever so earnestly for them.

O. HALLESBY

December 15

This is the God-given revelation: that when we are born again of the Spirit of God and indwelt by the Holy Spirit, He intercedes for us with a tenderness and an understanding akin to the Lord Jesus Christ and akin to God, that is, He expresses the unutterable for us.

O. CHAMBERS

Ye have received the Spirit of adoption.

ROMANS 8:15

January 18

)f God is taking us into the understanding that prayer is for the glorifying of His Father, He will give us the first sign of His intimacy—silence. The devil calls it unanswered prayer.

O. CHAMBERS

Ye shall receive.
MATTHEW 21:22

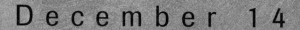

December 14

To pray is to let Jesus into our lives. He knocks and seeks admittance, not only in the solemn hours of secret prayer, He knocks in the midst of your daily work, your daily struggles, your daily "grind." That is when you need Him most.

O. HALLESBY

January 19

Think of the deep consciousness that God's almighty grace has effected something in us, to prove that we really bear His image and are fitted for a life of communion with Him and prepared to glorify Him. Think how we...may manifest something of the character of our Lord Jesus in the holy fellowship with His Father which He had when on earth.

A. MURRAY

December 13

It is comparatively easy to wait upon God; but to wait upon Him only—to feel, so far as our strength, happiness, and usefulness are concerned, as if all creatures and second causes were annihilated and we were alone in the universe with God is, I suspect, a difficult and rare attainment.

E. M. BOUNDS

J a n u a r y   2 0

As impossible as it is for us to take a breath in the morning large enough to last us until noon, so impossible is it to pray in the morning in such a way as to last us until noon. Let your prayers ascend to Him constantly, audibly or silently, as circumstances throughout the day permit.

O. HALLESBY

Pray without ceasing.
1 THESSALONIANS 5:17

December 12

I beseech you, do not think little of the grace that you have a holy God who longs to make you holy. Do not think little of the voice of God which calls you to give time to Him in the stillness of the inner chamber, so that He may cause His holiness to rest on you.

A. MURRAY

Be ye holy; for I am holy.

1 PETER 1:16

January 21

I feel it is far better to begin with God, to see His face first, to get my soul near Him before it is near another. In general it is best to have at least one hour alone with God before engaging in anything else.

E. M. BOUNDS

His compassions fail not. They are new every morning: great is thy faithfulness.
LAMENTATIONS 3:22-23

December 11

*P*rayer is God's answer to our poverty, not a power we exercise to obtain an answer.

O. CHAMBERS

Blessed are the poor in spirit:
for theirs is the kingdom of heaven.

MATTHEW 5:3

January 22

One wonderful thing about God's stillness in connection with your prayers is that He makes you still, makes you perfectly confident, the contagion of Jesus Christ's stillness gets into you—"I know He has heard me"—and His silence is the proof He has heard.

O. CHAMBERS

And I knew that thou hearest me always.
JOHN 11:42

December 10

*G*od is merciful even when He declines to give us things that we ask of Him.

O. HALLESBY

Thou hast covered thyself with a cloud, that our prayer should not pass through.

LAMENTATIONS 3:44

January 23

While others still slept, He went away to pray and to renew His strength in communion with His Father. He had need of this, otherwise He would not have been ready for the new day. The holy work of delivering souls demands constant renewal through fellowship with God.

A. MURRAY

And in the morning, rising up a great while before day, he went out, and departed into a solitary place, and there prayed.

MARK 1:35

December 9

*G*od is always within call, it is true; His ear is ever attentive to the cry of His child, but we can never get to know Him if we use the vehicle of prayer as we use the telephone—for a few words of hurried conversation. Intimacy requires development. We can never know God as it is our privilege to know Him by brief repetitions that are requests for personal favors and nothing more. That is not the way in which we can come into communication with heaven's King.

E. M. BOUNDS

J a n u a r y 2 4

*P*rayer fails when the desire and effort for personal holiness fail.

E. M. BOUNDS

Search me, O God, and know my heart.
PSALM 139:23

December 8

This is the glory of the inner chamber, to converse with God the Holy One.

A. MURRAY

They rest not day and night, saying, Holy, holy, holy, Lord God Almighty.

REVELATION 4:8

January 25

All work takes time. When it becomes clear to us that prayer is a part of our daily program of work, it will also become clear to us that we must arrange our daily program in such a way that there is time also for this work, just as we set aside time for other necessary things, such as eating and dressing.

O. HALLESBY

December 7

*I*n our praying we draw on our memories,
on our past experiences, on our present
desires. We only learn to draw on the grace
of God by pureness, by knowledge,
by long-suffering.

O. CHAMBERS

My prayer is pure.

JOB 16:17

J a n u a r y   2 6

$\mathcal{G}$od does not give faith in answer to prayer:
He reveals himself in answer to prayer, and
faith is exercised spontaneously.

O. CHAMBERS

Let him ask in faith.

JAMES 1:6

December 6

The goal of prayer is the ear of God, a goal that can only be reached by patient and continued and continuous waiting upon Him, pouring out our heart to Him, and permitting Him to speak to us.... As we come to know Him better we shall spend more time in His presence and find that presence a constant and ever-increasing delight.

E. M. BOUNDS

In thy presence is fulness of joy.
PSALM 16:11

J a n u a r y   2 7

The entire day receives order and discipline when it acquires unity. This unity must be sought and found in morning prayer. The morning prayer determines the day.

D. BONHOEFFER

Cause me to hear thy lovingkindness
in the morning.

PSALM 143:8

December 5

We impoverish God in our minds when we say there must be answers to our prayers on the material plane; the biggest answers to our prayers are in the realm of the unseen.

O. CHAMBERS

Look not at the things which are seen.

2 CORINTHIANS 4:18

J a n u a r y   3 0

The greatest answer to prayer is that I am brought into a perfect understanding with God, and that alters my view of actual things.

O. CHAMBERS

December 2

What God wills to accomplish on earth needs prayer as its indispensable condition. And there is but one way for Christ and believers. A heart and mouth open toward heaven in believing prayer will certainly not be put to shame.

A. MURRAY

Fear not; for thou shalt not be ashamed.

ISAIAH 54:4

January 29

*I*f we view prayer as a constant fellowship, an unbroken audience with the King, it then loses every vestige of dread which it may once have possessed; we regard it no longer as a duty which must be performed, but rather as a privilege which is to be enjoyed, a rare delight that is always revealing some new beauty.

E. M. BOUNDS

Let us come before his presence with thanksgiving.

PSALM 95:2

December 3

The more helpless you are, the better you are fitted to pray, and the more answers to prayer you will experience.

O. HALLESBY

January 31

In the Great House of God there is a furnace. This furnace affects the whole house, and your prayers fuel the furnace. Your intercession is coal on the fire. Your pleadings are kindling to the flames. The furnace is sturdy, the vents are ready; all that is needed is your prayer.

MAX LUCADO

December 1

The Lord's Prayer is a floor plan of the house of God: a step-by-step description of how God meets our needs when we dwell in Him. Everything that occurs in a healthy house is described in this prayer. Protection, instruction, forgiveness, provision...all occur under God's roof.

MAX LUCADO

February 1

The soul which has come into intimate contact with God in the silence of the prayer chamber is never out of conscious touch with the Father; the heart is always going out to Him in loving communion, and the moment the mind is released from the task upon which it is engaged, it returns as naturally to God as the bird does to its nest. What a beautiful conception of prayer we get if we regard it in this light.

E. M. BOUNDS

November 30

In God's name, I beseech you, let prayer nourish your soul as your meals nourish your body. Let your fixed seasons of prayer keep you in God's presence through the day, and His presence frequently remembered...an ever-fresh spring of prayer.

E. M. BOUNDS

Peter and John went up together into the temple at the hour of prayer.

ACTS 3:1

February 2

*D*o you long to know how you may always experience deliverance from the sin of prayerlessness? Here you have the secret. Believe in the Son of God, give Him time in the inner chamber to reveal himself in His ever present nearness, as the Eternal and Almighty One, the Eternal Love who watches over you.... It has not entered into the heart of man what God can do for those who love Him.

A. MURRAY

November 29

We are ill-taught if we look for results only in the earthlies when we pray. A praying saint performs far more havoc among the unseen forces of darkness than we have the slightest notion of.

O. CHAMBERS

We wrestle not against flesh and blood.

EPHESIANS 6:12

February 3

The purpose of fasting is to loosen to some degree the ties which bind us to the world of material things and our surroundings as a whole, in order that we may concentrate all our spiritual powers upon the unseen and eternal things.

O. HALLESBY

This kind goeth not out but by prayer and fasting.

MATTHEW 17:21

November 28

We can never expect to grow in the likeness of our Lord unless we follow His example and give more time to communion with the Father.

E. M. BOUNDS

I will behold thy face in righteousness:
I shall be satisfied, when I awake,
with thy likeness.

PSALM 17:15

February 4

Our Lord never referred to unanswered prayer; He taught that prayers were always answered. He ever implied that prayers were answered rightly because of the Heavenly Father's wisdom.

O. CHAMBERS

Whatsoever we ask, we receive of him.
1 JOHN 3:22

November 27

*I*t is blessed to know of a place where we can lay our tired head and heart, our heavenly Father's arms, and say to Him, "I can do no more. And I have nothing to tell you. May I lie here a while and rest? Everything will soon be well again if I can only rest in Your arms a while."

O. HALLESBY

My beloved spake, and said…
Rise up, my love…and come away.
SONG OF SOLOMON 2:10

February 5

*P*rayer is the helpless and needy child crying to the compassion of the Father's heart and the bounty and power of a Father's hand. The answer is as sure to come as the Father's heart can be touched and the Father's hand moved.

E. M. BOUNDS

O Lord, attend unto my cry,
give ear unto my prayer.

PSALM 17:1

November 26

The great lesson for every prayer is—see to it, first of all, that you commit yourself to the leading of the Holy Spirit, and with entire dependence on Him, give Him the first place. For through Him your prayer will have a value you cannot imagine, and through Him also you will learn to speak out your desires in the name of Christ.

A. MURRAY

As many as are led by the Spirit of God,
they are the sons of God.

ROMANS 8:14

February 6

*I*t is not only blessed to give thanks; it is also of vital importance to our prayer life in general. If we have noted the Lord's answers to our prayers and thanked Him for what we have received of Him, then it becomes easier for us, and we get more courage, to pray for more.

O. HALLESBY

Let us offer the sacrifice of praise to God continually.

HEBREWS 13:15

November 25

A most beneficial exercise in secret prayer before the Father is to write things down so that I see exactly what I think and want to say. Only those who have tried these ways know the ineffable benefit of such strenuous times in secret.

O. CHAMBERS

February 7

*I*f our petitions are in accordance with His will, and if we seek His glory in the asking, the answers will come in ways that will astonish us and fill our hearts with songs of thanksgiving.

J. K. MACLEAN

I will praise the name of God with a song,
and will magnify him with thanksgiving.

PSALM 69:30

November 24

*I*t is not our prayer which draws Jesus into our hearts. Nor is it our prayer which moves Jesus to come in to us. All He needs is access. He enters in of His own accord, because He desires to come in. And He enters in wherever He is not denied admittance.

O. HALLESBY

If any man hear my voice,
and open the door, I will come in.

REVELATION 3:20

February 8

*L*abor at prayer! There is nothing thrilling about a laboring man's work, but it is the laboring man who makes the conceptions of the genius possible; and it is the laboring saint who makes the conception of his Master possible.

O. CHAMBERS

November 23

*G*od's willingness to answer our prayers exceeds our willingness to give good and necessary things to our children, just as far as God's ability, goodness, and perfection exceed our infirmities and evil.

E. M. BOUNDS

How much more shall your Father which is in heaven give good things to them that ask him?

MATTHEW 7:11

February 9

*J*esus taught that perseverance is the essential element of prayer. Men must be in earnest when they kneel at God's footstool. Too often we get faint-hearted and quit praying at the point where we ought to begin. We let go at the very point where we should hold on strongest.

E. M. BOUNDS

Ask in faith, nothing wavering.

JAMES 1:6

November 22

The first and the decisive battle in connection with prayer is the conflict which arises when we are to make arrangements to be alone with God every day. If the battle is lost for any length of time at this point, the enemy has already won the first skirmish.

O. HALLESBY

I have called daily upon thee.

PSALM 88:9

February 10

It is Jesus who comes to meet us in the inner chamber and gives the positive assurance that unbroken fellowship with Him is our inheritance and will, through Him, become our experience.

A. MURRAY

Herein is love, not that we loved God, but that he loved us, and sent his Son.

1 JOHN 4:10

November 21

The battle of prayer is against two things in the earthlies: wandering thoughts, and lack of intimacy with God's character as revealed in His word. Neither can be cured at once, but they can be cured by discipline.

O. CHAMBERS

February 11

When you enter your secret chamber, take plenty of time before you begin to speak. Let quietude wield its influence upon you. Let the fact that you are alone assert itself. Give your soul time to get released from the many outward things. Give God time to play the prelude to prayer for the benefit of your distracted soul.

O. HALLESBY

November 20

*M*ake mine (statue) kneeling, for thus
I came to glory.

CROMWELL

*Whatsoever ye shall ask in my name, that
will I do, that the Father may be glorified.*

JOHN 14:13

February 12

*P*rayer imparts the power to walk and not faint.

O. CHAMBERS

They that wait upon the Lord shall renew their strength...they shall walk, and not faint.

ISAIAH 40:31

November 19

It is the will of our heavenly Father that we should come to Him freely and confidently and make known our desires to Him, just as we would have our children come freely and of their own accord and speak to us about the things they would like to have.

O. HALLESBY

When ye pray, say, Our Father...give us day by day our daily bread.

LUKE 11:2–3

February 13

*J*ust as an earthly father knows what is best for his children's welfare, so does God take into consideration the particular needs of His human family, and meets them out of His wonderful storehouse.

J. K. MACLEAN

I will…open you the windows of heaven, and pour you out a blessing, that there shall not be room enough to receive it.
MALACHI 3:10

November 18

Around us is a world lost in sin, above us is a God willing and able to save; it is ours to build the bridge that links heaven and earth, and prayer is the mighty instrument that does the work. If we do our part, God will do His.

E. M. BOUNDS

When he saw the multitudes, he was moved with compassion.

MATTHEW 9:36

February 14

*I*t is necessary for the Spirit of God to burn into our hearts this mystery, that the most important work we have to do is that which must be done on our knees, alone with God, away from the bustle of the world and the plaudits of men.

O. HALLESBY

November 17

*P*rayer is not logical, it is a mysterious moral working of the Holy Spirit.

O. CHAMBERS

Unto you it is given to know the mystery of the kingdom of God.

MARK 4:11

February 15

*P*ray and never faint, is the motto Christ gives us for praying. It is the test of our faith, and the more severe the trial and the longer the waiting, the more glorious the results.

E. M. BOUNDS

November 16

*I*t is clear that success in prayer does not depend upon the assurance of the one who prays, nor upon his boldness, nor any such thing, but upon this one thing, that he opens his heart to Jesus.

O. HALLESBY

It is the voice of my beloved that knocketh, saying, Open to me.

SONG OF SOLOMON 5:2

February 16

When we lean to our own understanding
we do away with prayer and bank all on service.
Consequently by succeeding in the external we
fail in the eternal. In the eternal we succeed
only by prevailing prayer.

O. CHAMBERS

November 15

*P*rayer is of transcendent importance. Prayer is the mightiest agent to advance God's work. Praying hearts and hands only can do God's work. Prayer succeeds when all else fails.

E. M. Bounds

Pray always, that ye may be accounted worthy.

LUKE 21:36

February 17

✝he incarnate Son of God has borne every human weakness in His own flesh; He pours out the heart of all humanity before God and stands in our place and prays for us.

D. BONHOEFFER

He ever liveth to make intercession for them.

HEBREWS 7:25

November 14

Would that we might learn from our Lord
Jesus how impossible it is to walk with God, to
obtain God's blessing or leading, or to do His
work joyously and fruitfully, apart from close
unbroken fellowship with Him who is ever a
living fountain of spiritual life and power!

A. MURRAY

He that abideth in me, and I in him,
the same bringeth forth much fruit.

JOHN 15:5

February 18

Importunity is a condition of prayer. We are to press the matter, not with vain repetitions, but with urgent repetitions. We repeat, not to count the times, but to gain the prayer. We cannot quit praying because heart and soul are in it. We pray "with all perseverance." We hang on to our prayers because by them we live. We press our pleas because we must have them or die.

E. M. BOUNDS

November 13

When a man is at his wits' end it is not a cowardly thing to pray, it is the only way he can get in touch with Reality.

O. CHAMBERS

Hear my prayer, O Lord,
and give ear unto my cry.

PSALM 39:12

February 19

Wherever we go, we meet people who are in need of something. If the Spirit could give us that open eye of love which sees both visible and invisible needs, everything we saw would give rise to prayer.

O. HALLESBY

Let my prayer be set forth before thee as incense.

PSALM 141:2

November 12

*P*raying men are God's chosen leaders. The distinction between the leaders that God brings to the front to lead and bless His people, and those leaders who owe their position of leadership to a worldly, selfish, unsanctified selection, is this: God's leaders are pre-eminently men of prayer.

E. M. BOUNDS

February 20

Without our intercession someone will be impoverished. Let us remember the depth and height and solemnity of our calling as saints.

O. CHAMBERS

And he saw that there was no man, and wondered that there was no intercessor.

ISAIAH 59:16

November 11

*P*rayer can assume very different forms, from quiet, blessed contemplation of God, in which eye meets eye in restful meditation, to deep sighs or sudden exclamations of wonder, joy, gratitude, or adoration.

O. HALLESBY

Serve the Lord with gladness: come before his presence with singing.

PSALM 100:2

February 21

*T*ake time in the inner chamber to bow down and worship; and wait on Him till He unveils himself, and takes possession of you, and goes out with you to show how a man may live and walk in abiding fellowship with an unseen Lord.

A. MURRAY

*Come before him: worship
the Lord in the beauty of holiness.*

1 CHRONICLES 16:29

November 10

Of all the duties enjoined by Christianity none is more essential and yet more neglected than prayer.

F. FÉNELON

Men ought always to pray, and not to faint.

LUKE 18:1

February 22

Our lives should be, according to our Lord's plans, quiet but steadily flowing streams of blessing, which through our prayers and intercessions should reach our whole environment.

O. HALLESBY

Out of his belly
shall flow rivers of living water.
JOHN 7:38

November 9

We have not the remotest conception of what is done by our prayers, nor have we the right to try and examine and understand it; all we know is that Jesus Christ laid all stress on prayer.

O. CHAMBERS

I do nothing of myself;
but as my Father hath taught me.

JOHN 8:28

February 23

*H*eart, soul, life must be in our praying; the heavens must feel the force of our crying, and must be brought into oppressed sympathy for our bitter and needy state. A need that oppresses us, and has no relief but in our crying to God, must voice our praying.

E. M. BOUNDS

I have heard thy prayer,
I have seen thy tears.

2 KINGS 20:5

November 8

)f we pray for anything according to the will of God, we already have what we pray for the moment we ask it. We do not know exactly when it will arrive; but we have learned to know God through the Spirit of God, and have learned to leave this in His hands, and to live just as happily whether the answer arrives immediately or later.

O. HALLESBY

Before they call, I will answer; and while they are yet speaking, I will hear.

ISAIAH 65:24

February 24

*B*y intercessory prayer we can hold off
Satan from other lives and give the Holy
Ghost a chance with them. No wonder Jesus
put such tremendous emphasis on prayer!

O. CHAMBERS

Praying always for you.
COLOSSIANS 1:3

November 7

*J*esus was able to meet the enemy full
of courage, and in the power of God, gave
himself over to the death of the cross.
He had prayed.

A. MURRAY

*He went a little further, and fell on his
face, and prayed, saying...nevertheless not
as I will, but as thou wilt.*

MATTHEW 26:39

February 25

*J*esus wants to pray with us and to have us pray with Him, so that we may be confident and glad that God hears us. When our will wholeheartedly enters into the prayer of Christ, then we pray correctly...and with Him we also know that we shall be heard.

D. BONHOEFFER

If we know that he hears us...we know that we have the petitions that we desired of him.
1 JOHN 5:15

November 6

The great need of the Church in this and all ages is men of such commanding faith, of such unsullied holiness, of such marked spiritual vigor and consuming zeal, that they will work spiritual revolutions through their mighty praying.

E. M. BOUNDS

February 26

Our prayer chamber should have our freshest strength, our calmest time, its hours unfettered, without obtrusion, without haste. Private place and plenty of time are the life of prayer.

E. M. Bounds

November 5

You say, "But He has not answered." He has, He is so near to you that His silence is the answer. His silence is big with terrific meaning that you cannot understand yet, but presently you will.

O. CHAMBERS

And after the fire a still small voice.

1 KINGS 19:12

February 27

*I*t is only when we pray for something according to the will of God that we have the promise of being heard and answered.

O. HALLESBY

If we ask any thing according to his will, he heareth us.

1 JOHN 5:14

N o v e m b e r   4

There is neither encouragement nor room in Bible religion for feeble desires, listless efforts, lazy attitudes; all must be strenuous, urgent, ardent. Inflamed desires, impassioned, unwearied insistence delight heaven. God would have His children incorrigibly in earnest and persistently bold in their efforts. Heaven is too busy to listen to half-hearted prayers or to respond to pop-calls. Our whole being must be in our praying.

E. M. BOUNDS

February 28

*E*very time we pray our horizon is altered, our attitude to things is altered, not sometimes but every time, and the amazing thing is that we don't pray more.

O. CHAMBERS

Praying always with all prayer.
EPHESIANS 6:18

November 3

There come times when I have nothing more to tell God. If I were to continue to pray in words, I would have to repeat what I have already said. At such times it is wonderful to say to God, "May I be in Thy presence, Lord? I have nothing more to say to Thee, but I do love to be in Thy presence."

O. HALLESBY

I sought him whom my soul loveth.
SONG OF SOLOMON 3:1

February 29

*P*rayer in its highest form and grandest success assumes the attitude of a wrestler with God. It is the contest, trial, and victory of faith; a victory not secured from an enemy, but from Him who tries our faith that He may enlarge it: that tests our strength to make us stronger. Few things give such quickened and permanent vigor to the soul as a long exhaustive season of importunate prayer.

E. M. BOUNDS

November 2

Your walk with God is essential. His heart
is not seen in an occasional chat or weekly
visit. We learn His will as we take up
residence in His house every single day.

MAX LUCADO

March 1

There are times when to speak is to violate the moment...when silence represents the highest respect. The word for such times is reverence. The prayer for such times is "Hallowed be thy name."

MAX LUCADO

November 1

Prayer is often a temptation to bank on a miracle of God…it is much easier to ask God to do my work than it is to do it myself. Until we are disciplined properly, we will always be inclined to bank on God's miracles and refuse to do the moral thing ourselves. It is our job, and it will never be done unless we do it.

O. CHAMBERS

March 2

Whenever we touch His almighty arm, some of His omnipotence streams in upon us, into our souls and into our bodies. And not only that, but, through us, it streams out to others.

O. HALLESBY

October 31

*n*o matter in what distress we may be, distress of body or of soul, we need but look unto Him who is always near with that healing power which can immediately overcome the death-dealing poison of sin and its terrible consequences both to body and soul.

O. HALLESBY

And it shall come to pass, that every one...who looketh upon it, shall live.

NUMBERS 21:8

March 3

*n*ever say you will pray about a thing;
pray about it.

O. CHAMBERS

October 30

All the true revivals have been born in prayer. When God's people become so concerned about the state of religion that they lie on their faces day and night in earnest supplication, the blessing will be sure to fall.

E. M. BOUNDS

If my people...shall humble themselves,
and pray, and seek my face...then will I hear
from heaven, and will forgive their sin,
and will heal their land.

2 CHRONICLES 7:14

March 4

*I*f I bow before Him in my inner chamber, then I am in contact with the eternal, unchanging power of God. If I commit myself for the day to the Lord Jesus, then I may rest assured that it is His eternal, almighty power which has taken me under its protection and which will accomplish everything for me.

A. MURRAY

In thy faithfulness answer me.
PSALM 143:1

October 29

*G*od's object is to encourage faith and to make His children and servants see that they must take trouble to understand and rely upon the unspeakable greatness and omnipotence of God, so that they may take literally and in a childlike spirit this word: "Unto Him that is able to do exceeding abundantly above all that we ask or think...be glory throughout all ages."

A. MURRAY

March 5

It is God's will not only to hear our prayer, but to give us the best and the richest answer which He, the almighty and omniscient God, can devise. He will send us the answer when it will benefit us and His cause the most.

O. HALLESBY

My prayer is unto thee, O Lord,
in an acceptable time.

PSALM 69:13

October 28

Quit praying about yourself, and be spent in vicarious intercession as the bondslave of Jesus.

O. CHAMBERS

He must increase, but I must decrease.

JOHN 3:30

March 6

We must live for God out of the closet if we would meet God in the closet. It is what we are out of the closet which gives victory or brings defeat to the closet. If the spirit of the world prevails in our non-closet hours, the spirit of the world will prevail in our closet hours, and that will be a vain and idle farce.

E. M. BOUNDS

October 27

Praying which does not result in pure conduct is a delusion. We have missed the whole office and virtue of praying if it does not rectify conduct. It is in the very nature of things that we must quit praying or quit bad conduct.

E. M. BOUNDS

Whatsoever we ask, we receive of him, because we keep his commandments.

1 JOHN 3:22

March 7

*P*rayer is not a question of altering things externally, but of working wonders in a man's disposition.

O. CHAMBERS

I will walk at liberty:
for I seek thy precepts.
PSALM 119:45

October 26

*H*elplessness is unquestionably the first and the surest indication of a praying heart. As far as I can see, prayer has been ordained only for the helpless. Prayer and helplessness are inseparable. Only he who is helpless can truly pray.

O. HALLESBY

For we know not what we should pray for.

ROMANS 8:26

March 8

Be not afraid to pray; to pray is right;
Pray if thou canst with hope, but ever pray,
Though hope be weak or sick with long delay;
Pray in the darkness if there be no light;
And if for any wish thou dare not pray,
Then pray to God to cast that wish away.

October 25

*P*rayer is not merely coming to God to ask something from Him. It is above all fellowship with God and being brought under the power of His holiness and love, till He takes possession of us and stamps our entire nature with the lowliness of Christ, which is the secret of all true worship.

A. MURRAY

I am meek and lowly in heart.
MATTHEW 11:29

March 9

Importunity is made up of the ability to hold on, to press on, to wait with unrelaxed and unrelaxable grasp, restless desire, and restful patience. Importunate prayer is not an incident but the main thing, not a performance but a passion, not a need but a necessity.

E. M. BOUNDS

Because of his importunity he will rise....
Knock, and it shall be opened unto you.
LUKE 11:8-9

October 24

The meaning of prayer is that I bring power to bear upon another soul that is weak enough to yield and strong enough to resist; hence the need for strenuous intercessory prayer.

O. CHAMBERS

March 10

Our prayer life will become restful when it really dawns upon us that we have done all we are supposed to do when we have spoken to Him about it. From that moment we have left it with Him. It is His responsibility.

O. HALLESBY

God hath heard me.

PSALM 66:19

October 23

When we in prayer seek only the glorification of the name of God, then we are in complete harmony with the Spirit of prayer. Then our hearts are at rest both while we pray and after we have prayed. Then we can wait for the Lord.

O. HALLESBY

I wait for the Lord…
and in his word do I hope.

PSALM 130:5

March 11

*I*n prayer have we learned the wonderful power of that phrase "boldness to enter into the holiest by the blood of Jesus"? It means that we can talk to God as Jesus Christ did, but only through the right of His atonement.

O. CHAMBERS

October 22

Only praying hands can build for God.
They are God's mighty ones on earth, His
master-builders.

E. M. BOUNDS

Building up yourselves on your most holy
faith, praying in the Holy Ghost.

JUDE 1:20

March 12

*P*rayer is our most formidable weapon; the thing which makes all else we do efficient.

E. M. Bounds

Praying always with all prayer and supplication in the Spirit.

EPHESIANS 6:18

October 21

*I*n the midst of all our zeal in the work of the Church, of all our faithfulness in preaching and conversation with the people, we lack that ceaseless prayer which has attached to it the sure promise of the Spirit and the power from on high.

A. MURRAY

Tarry...until ye be endued with power from on high.

LUKE 24:49

March 13

As we learn to know Jesus, our prayers become quiet, confidential, and blessed conversations with Him, our best friend, about the things that are on our minds.

O. HALLESBY

Lord, to whom shall we go?
thou hast the words of eternal life.

JOHN 6:68

October 20

The whole meaning of prayer is that we may know God.

O. CHAMBERS

That I may know him.

PHILIPPIANS 3:10

March 14

The child learns to speak because his father speaks to him. He learns the speech of his father. So we learn to speak to God because God has spoken to us and speaks to us. By means of the speech of the Father in heaven His children learn to speak with Him. Repeating God's own words after Him, we begin to pray to Him.

D. BONHOEFFER

As he was praying in a certain place, when he ceased, one of his disciples said unto him, Lord, teach us to pray.

LUKE 11:1

October 19

If we will make use of prayer to call down upon ourselves and others those things which will glorify the name of God, then we shall see the strongest and boldest promises of the Bible about prayer fulfilled. Then we shall see such answers to prayer as we had never thought were possible.

O. HALLESBY

Call unto me, and I will answer thee,
and shew thee great and mighty things,
which thou knowest not.

JEREMIAH 33:3

March 15

*P*rayer is the supreme activity of all that is noblest in our personality, and the essential nature of prayer is faith.

O. CHAMBERS

Without faith it is impossible to please him:
for he that cometh to God
must believe that he is.

HEBREWS 11:6

October 18

*n*atural ability and educational advantages do not figure as factors in this matter of prayer; but a capacity for faith, the power of a thorough consecration, the ability of self-littleness, an absolute losing of one's self in God's glory, and an ever-present and insatiable yearning and seeking after all the fullness of God.

E. M. BOUNDS

March 16

*P*rayer is the easiest and hardest of all things; the simplest and the sublimest; the weakest and the most powerful; its results lie outside the range of human possibilities—they are limited only by the omnipotence of God.

E. M. BOUNDS

October 17

Our enemies will pursue us deliberately into our very prayer rooms. The only way in which we can gather and keep collected our distracted minds and our roaming thoughts is to center them about Jesus Christ. By that I mean that we should let Christ lay hold of, attract, captivate, and gather about himself all our interests. Then our sessions of prayer will become real meetings with God.

O. HALLESBY

March 17

The Lord Jesus, who in His love is so unspeakably near us, is the Almighty One with whom nothing is impossible. Everything that is promised in God's Word, all that is our inheritance as children of the New Covenant, the Almighty Jesus can bestow upon us.

A. MURRAY

All the promises of God in him are yea, and in him Amen.

2 CORINTHIANS 1:20

October 16

There is nothing to be valued more highly than to have people praying for us; God links up His power in answer to their prayers.

O. CHAMBERS

Brethren, pray for us, that the word of the Lord may have free course.

2 THESSALONIANS 3:1

March 18

Nothing is so blessed as quiet, unbroken communication with our Lord. The sense of the Lord's nearness, which then fills our souls, is greater than any other peace, joy, inner satisfaction, or security which we have known.

O. HALLESBY

October 15

Communion alone with God...
the Spirit's trysting hours of heavenly love.

E. M. BOUNDS

He went up into a mountain apart to prayer...he was there alone.

MATTHEW 14:23

March 19

The inattentive, slovenly way we drift into the presence of God is an indication that we are not bothering to think about Him. Whenever our Lord spoke of prayer, He said, "Ask." It is impossible to ask if you do not concentrate.

O. CHAMBERS

Ask, and it shall be given you.

LUKE 11:9

October 14

The Spirit of prayer will not only show you the true meaning and purpose of prayer; He will also lift you in all your helplessness up to the very heart of God where you will be warmed by His love, so that you can begin to pray according to His will, asking for nothing except those things which are in harmony with His plans and purposes.

O. HALLESBY

March 20

If we are to pray aright, perhaps it is quite necessary that we pray contrary to our own heart. Not what we want to pray is important, but what God wants us to pray. The richness of the Word of God ought to determine our prayer, not the poverty of our heart.

D. BONHOEFFER

October 13

The potency of prayer hath subdued the strength of fire; it had bridled the rage of lions, hushed anarchy to rest, extinguished wars, appeased the elements, expelled demons, burst the chains of death, expanded the gates of heaven, assuaged diseases, repelled frauds, rescued cities from destruction, stayed the sun in its course, and arrested the progress of the thunderbolt.

CHRYSOSTOM

March 21

We need to learn to know Him so well that we feel safe when we have left our difficulties with Him. To know Jesus in that way is a prerequisite of all true prayer.

O. HALLESBY

He will regard the prayer of the destitute.

PSALM 102:17

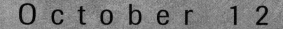

October 12

The revelation of our spiritual standing is what we ask in prayer; sometimes what we ask is an insult to God; we ask with our eyes on the possibilities or on ourselves, not on Jesus Christ.

O. CHAMBERS

Looking unto Jesus the author and finisher of our faith.

HEBREWS 12:2

March 22

We can do nothing without prayer. All things can be done by importunate prayer. It surmounts or removes all obstacles, overcomes every resisting force, and gains its ends in the face of invincible hindrances.

E. M. BOUNDS

O woman, great is thy faith:
be it unto thee even as thou wilt.

MATTHEW 15:28

October 11

We can come before God and say to Him, "I do not have a right to pray because I do not have a truly prayerful heart. Much less do I have any right to receive what I ask for. But hear me, not for my sake, nor for the sake of my prayer, and not even because of my distress, for it is a result of my own sinfulness. But hear me for Jesus' sake."

O. HALLESBY

March 23

)f we rely on the Holy Spirit, we shall find that our prayers become more and more inarticulate; and when they are inarticulate, reverence grows deeper and deeper.

O. CHAMBERS

October 10

This is the way in which we all act about prayer. Conscious as we are of its importance, of its vital importance, we yet let the hours pass away as a blank.

E. M. BOUNDS

March 24

*J*esus Christ, in His divine personality, in that eternal love which led Him to the cross, longs to have fellowship with us every moment of the day and to keep us in the enjoyment of that fellowship.

A. MURRAY

Now come I to thee...that they might have my joy fulfilled in themselves.

JOHN 17:13

October 9

The holy and most glorious God invites us to come to Him, to converse with Him, to ask from Him such things as we need, and to experience what a blessing there is in fellowship with Him. He has created us in His own image and has redeemed us by His own Son, so that in prayer with Him we might find our highest glory and salvation.

A. MURRAY

March 25

*I*f we would have God in the closet, God must have us out of the closet. There is no way of praying to God, but by living to God.

E. M. BOUNDS

October 8

*I*f we are struggling in prayer it is because the wiles of the enemy are getting the upper hand, and we must look for the cause of it in the lack of discipline in ourselves.

O. CHAMBERS

Put on the whole armour of God.

EPHESIANS 6:11

March 26

The Spirit of prayer would teach us that we should disregard the question as to whether the fulfillment of our prayer is hard or easy for God. What we think or do not think about this has no bearing on the hearing and answering of prayer.

O. HALLESBY

Hear my voice, O God, in my prayer.

PSALM 64:1

October 7

All that Christ has may become ours if we obey the conditions. The one secret is prayer. The place of revealing and of equipping, of grace and of power, is the prayer chamber, and as we meet there with God we shall not only win our triumphs, but we shall also grow in the likeness of our Lord and become His living witnesses to men.

E. M. BOUNDS

To be conformed to the image of his Son.

ROMANS 8:29

March 27

*S*ome of the qualities of God must be merged into us before our prayers can be fit for His acceptance.

O. CHAMBERS

*Let my cry come near before thee,
O Lord: give me understanding
according to thy word.*

PSALM 119:169

October 6

*J*esus wills of His own accord to come into us and, in His own power, to deal with our needs. It is not necessary for us to constrain Him by our prayers to take an interest in us.

O. HALLESBY

March 28

When thou feelest thyself most indisposed to prayer yield not to it, but strive and endeavor to pray even when thou thinkest thou canst not pray.

HILDERSAM

When my soul fainted within me...
my prayer came in unto thee.

JONAH 2:7

October 5

Live in what must be. Do not live in your human imagination of what is possible. Live in the Word—in the love and infinite faithfulness of the Lord Jesus. The faith that always thanks Him—not for experiences, but for the promises on which it can rely.

A. MURRAY

Great is thy faithfulness.... The Lord is good unto them that wait for him.

LAMENTATIONS 3:23,25

March 29

A humble and contrite heart knows that it can merit nothing before God, and that all that is necessary is to be reconciled to one's helplessness and let our holy and almighty God care for us, just as an infant surrenders himself to his mother's care.

O. HALLESBY

To this man will I look, even to him
that is poor and of a contrite spirit.

ISAIAH 66:2

October 4

*G*od's "nothings" are His most positive answers. We have to stay on God and wait. Never try to help God to fulfill His word.

O. CHAMBERS

Tarry ye here, and watch.

MARK 14:34

March 30

*P*rayer is mighty in its operations, and God never disappoints those who put their trust and confidence in Him. They may have to wait long for the answer, and they may not live to see it, but the prayer of faith never misses its object.

E. M. BOUNDS

If ye shall ask any thing
in my name, I will do it.

JOHN 14:14

October 3

As soon as the Spirit has taught us to pray in the name of Jesus, He will teach us plainly that what we lack in fervency, solicitude, love, and faith are not the things which prevent us from being heard and answered when we pray. These things merely reveal our helplessness.

O. HALLESBY

March 31

We realize that we are energized by the Holy Spirit for prayer, we know what it is to pray in the atmosphere and the presence of the Holy Spirit; but we do not so often realize that the Holy Spirit himself prays in us with prayers that we cannot utter.

O. CHAMBERS

Who also maketh intercession for us.
ROMANS 8:34

October 2

*y*ou can talk to God because God listens. Your voice matters in heaven. He takes you very seriously. When you enter His presence, the attendants turn to you to hear your voice. No need to fear that you will be ignored. Even if you stammer or stumble, even if what you have to say impresses no one, it impresses God—and He listens.

MAX LUCADO

April 1

When you are confused about the future, go to your Jehovah-raah, your caring shepherd. When you are anxious about provision, talk to Jehovah-jireh, the Lord who provides. Are your challenges too great? Seek the help of Jehovah-shalom, the Lord is peace. Is your body sick? Are your emotions weak? Jehovah-rophe, the Lord who heals you, will see you now. Do you feel like a soldier stranded behind enemy lines? Take refuge in Jehovah-nissi, the Lord my banner.

MAX LUCADO

October 1

The Christian life rooted in the secret place where God meets and walks and talks with His own grows into such a testimony of Divine power that all men will feel its influence and be touched by the warmth of its love.

E. M. BOUNDS

He that dwelleth in the secret place of the most High shall abide under the shadow of the Almighty.

PSALM 91:1

April 2

Love is the supreme condition of prayer, a life inspired by love. The law of love is the law of prayer.

E. M. BOUNDS

For ye yourselves are taught of God to love one another.

1 THESSALONIANS 4:9

September 30

*P*rayer is not an exercise, it is the life.

O. CHAMBERS

*In him we live, and move,
and have our being.*

ACTS 17:28

April 3

*B*e sure to remember that nothing in your daily life is so insignificant and so inconsequential that the Lord will not help you by answering your prayer.

O. HALLESBY

The very hairs of your head are all numbered.

MATTHEW 10:30

September 29

*G*od shapes the world by prayer. Prayers are deathless. The lips that uttered them may be closed in death, the heart that felt them may have ceased to beat, but the prayers live before God, and God's heart is set on them. Prayers outlive the lives of those who uttered them; outlive a generation, outlive an age, outlive a world.

E. M. BOUNDS

April 4

*P*rayer is simple, prayer is supernatural, and to anyone not related to our Lord Jesus Christ, prayer is apt to look stupid.

O. CHAMBERS

September 28

We should not be afraid, when praying to God, to give expression to a definite desire, even though we are in doubt at the time we are praying whether it is really the right thing to pray for or not.

O. HALLESBY

He shall give thee the desires
of thine heart.

PSALM 37:4

April 5

Christ taught us also to approach the Father in His name. That is our passport. It is in His name that we are to make our petitions known. That is the Divine declaration, and it opens up to every praying child a vista of infinite resource and possibility.

E. M. BOUNDS

Whatsoever ye shall ask the Father in my name, he will give it you.

JOHN 16:23

September 27

The great need of missions is the obtaining of men and women who will give themselves to the Lord to strive in prayer for the salvation of souls. God is eager and able to deliver and bless the world He has redeemed, if His people were but willing, if they were but ready, to cry to Him day and night.

A. MURRAY

Ask of me, and I shall give thee the heathen for thine inheritance.

PSALM 2:8

April 6

The Father knows that it is in our daily lives that we most easily become anxious. He knows, too, that our daily lives are made up of little things, not great things. Therefore He beckons to us in a friendly way and says, "Just bring all those little things to me; I am most willing to help you."

O. HALLESBY

Casting all your care upon him;
for he careth for you.
1 PETER 5:7

September 26

*L*et the Spirit of God teach you what He is driving at and learn not to grieve Him. If we are abiding in Jesus Christ we shall ask what He wants us to ask, whether we are conscious of doing so or not.

O. CHAMBERS

April 7

*H*ow did the Lord Jesus comfort His disciples? He promised that the Holy Spirit from heaven should so work in them a sense of the fullness of His life and of His personal presence that He would be even more intimately near and have more unbroken fellowship with them that they had ever experienced while He was upon the earth.

A. MURRAY

I will pray the Father,
and he shall give you another Comforter.
JOHN 14:16

September 25

*P*rayer is a condition of mind, an attitude of heart, which God recognizes as prayer whether it manifests itself in quiet thinking, in sighing, or in audible words.

O. HALLESBY

Let this mind be in you, which was also in Christ Jesus.

PHILIPPIANS 2:5

April 8

We think of prayer as a preparation for work, or a calm after having done work, whereas prayer is the essential work. It is the supreme activity of everything that is noblest in our personality.

O. CHAMBERS

September 24

I have resolved to pray more and pray always, to pray in all places where quietness inviteth, in the house, on the highway, and on the street; and to know no street or passage in this city that may not witness that I have not forgotten God.

SIR THOMAS BROWNE

April 9

A holy life does not live in the closet, but it cannot live without the closet.

E. M. BOUNDS

When thou prayest, enter into thy closet.

MATTHEW 6:6

September 23

Woe to the generation of sons who find their censers empty of the rich incense of prayer; whose fathers have been too busy or too unbelieving to pray. Perils inexpressible and consequences untold are their unhappy heritage. Fortunate are they whose fathers and mothers have left them a wealthy patrimony of prayer.

E. M. BOUNDS

April 10

*Y*ou can do more than pray after you have prayed, but you cannot do more than pray until you have prayed.

A. J. GORDON

Seek ye first the kingdom of God.
MATTHEW 6:33

September 22

We must get back to the place where we are concerned only about facing our own inner souls with Jesus Christ who searches us right down to the inmost recesses.

O. CHAMBERS

For the Lord searcheth all hearts.

1 CHRONICLES 28:9

April 11

We would not make so many rash and unspiritual choices, nor would we be so frequently at a loss what to do in the face of important decisions, if we would begin to fast in the Christian sense, and thus give the Spirit of prayer an opportunity to speak to our souls.

O. HALLESBY

September 21

*P*rayer strives after an intimate knowledge of God, rejoices in fellowship with Him, and then continues to lay hold of His strength. So, finally, it comes to this, "the flesh" must be denied and crucified.

A. MURRAY

I will love thee, O Lord, my strength.

PSALM 18:1

April 12

)narticulate prayer, the impulsive prayer that looks so futile, is the thing God always heeds. The habit of ejaculatory prayer ought to be the persistent habit of each one of us.

O. CHAMBERS

September 20

Jesus is moved to happiness every time He sees that you appreciate what He has done for you. Grip His pierced hand and say to Him, "I thank Thee, Savior, because Thou hast died for me." Thank Him likewise for all the other blessings He has showered upon you from day to day. It brings joy to Jesus.

O. HALLESBY

April 13

But faith will find its strength, not in the thought of what you will or do, but in the unchanging faithfulness and love of Christ, who has assured you, once again, that those who wait on Him shall not be ashamed.

A. MURRAY

Blessed be God, which hath
not turned away my prayer.

PSALM 66:20

September 19

*P*rayer introduced those who practiced it into a world of privilege, and brought the strength and wealth of heaven down to the aid of finite man. What rich and wonderful power was theirs who had learned the secret of victorious approach to God!

E. M. BOUNDS

April 14

To pray is nothing more involved than to open the door, giving Jesus access to our needs and permitting Him to exercise His own power in dealing with them.

O. HALLESBY

That God in all things may be glorified through Jesus Christ.

1 PETER 4:11

September 18

The greatest barrier to intercession is that we take ourselves so seriously and come to the conclusion that God is reserved with us; He is not. God has to ignore things we take so seriously until our relationship to Him is exactly that of a child.

O. CHAMBERS

Become as little children.
MATTHEW 18:3

April 15

*W*alking with God down the avenues of
prayer we acquire something of His likeness,
and unconsciously we become witnesses to
others of His beauty and His grace.

E. M. BOUNDS

September 17

See to it, night and day, that you pray for
your children. Then you will leave them a
great legacy of answers to prayer, which will
follow them all the days of their life. Then
you may calmly and with good conscience
depart from them, even though you may not
leave them a great deal of material wealth.

O. HALLESBY

April 16

So many of us limit our praying because we are not reckless in our confidence in God. In the eyes of those who do not know God, it is madness to trust Him, but when we pray in the Holy Ghost we begin to realize the resources of God, that He is our perfect heavenly Father, and we are His children.

O. CHAMBERS

In quietness and in confidence
shall be your strength.

ISAIAH 30:15

September 16

We cannot talk to God strongly when we have not lived for God strongly. The closet cannot be made holy to God when the life has not been holy to God.

E. M. BOUNDS

Create in me a clean heart, O God.

PSALM 51:10

April 17

*J*esus Christ has brought every need, every joy, every gratitude, every hope of men before God. He accompanies us, and brings us into the presence of God.

D. BONHOEFFER

No man cometh unto the Father, but by me.

JOHN 14:6

September 15

*I*t is a glorious thing to get to know God in a new way in the inner chamber. It is something still greater and more glorious to know God as the all-sufficient One and to wait on His Spirit to open our hearts and minds wide to receive the great things, the new things which He really longs to bestow on those who wait for Him.

A. MURRAY

Behold, I will do a new thing.

ISAIAH 43:19

April 18

I ought to spend the best hours of the day in communion with God.

E. M. BOUNDS

He went out into a mountain to pray,
and continued all night.

LUKE 6:12

September 14

*G*od engineers the circumstances of His saints
in order that the Spirit may use them as the
praying-house of the Son of God. If you are
spiritual the Holy Spirit is offering up prayers
in your bodily temple that you know nothing
about; it is the Spirit making intercession in you.

O. CHAMBERS

He ever liveth to make intercession.

HEBREWS 7:25

April 19

When prayer is a struggle, do not worry about the prayers that you cannot pray. You yourself are a prayer to God at that moment. All that is within you cries out to Him. And He hears all the pleas that your suffering soul and body are making to Him with groanings which cannot be uttered.

O. HALLESBY

September 13

*P*rayer is a mighty force, an energy that
moves heaven and pours untold treasures
of good on earth.

E. M. BOUNDS

When they had prayed,
the place was shaken.
ACTS 4:31

April 20

The only ground of our approach to God is "by the blood of Jesus" and by no other way. The one fundamental thing in prayer is the atoning work of Jesus Christ.

O. CHAMBERS

Having...boldness to enter into the holiest by the blood of Jesus.

HEBREWS 10:19

September 12

*T*he greatest transmission of God's power takes place through the believer's prayers and intercessions. Believing prayer is unquestionably the means by which God, in the quickest way, would be able to give to the world those saving powers from the realm of eternity which are necessary before Christ can return and the millennium be ushered in.

O. HALLESBY

April 21

The voice of the Father will be heard as He sets before us a widely opened door and receives us into blessed fellowship with himself. When we pray for the Spirit's help, it will no longer be in the fear that prayer is too great an effort for us. Instead, we will simply fall down at the Lord's feet in our weakness. There we will find the victory and power that comes from His love.

A. MURRAY

September 11

When we pray relying on the Holy Ghost, He will always bring us back to this one point, that we are not heard because we are in earnest, or because we need to be heard, or because we will perish if we are not heard; we are heard only on the ground of the atonement of our Lord.

O. CHAMBERS

April 22

To pray is to open the door unto Jesus and admit Him into your distress. Your helplessness is the very thing which opens wide the door unto Him and gives Him access to all your needs.

O. HALLESBY

O Lord, attend unto my cry,
give ear unto my prayer.

PSALM 17:1

September 10

The strongest one in Christ's Kingdom is he who is the best pray-er. The secret of success in Christ's Kingdom is the ability to pray. The one who can wield the power of prayer is the strong one, the holy one in Christ's Kingdom.

E. M. BOUNDS

I give myself unto prayer.

PSALM 109:4

April 23

*T*he prayer closet is the battlefield of the Church, the base of supplies for the Christian and the Church. Cut off from it there is nothing left but retreat and disaster.

E. M. BOUNDS

September 9

When we go to our meeting with God,
we should go like a patient to his doctor,
first to be thoroughly examined and
afterwards to be treated for our ailment.
Then something will happen when you pray.

O. HALLESBY

April 24

We have the idea that prayer is for special times, but we have to put on the armor of God for the continual practice of prayer, so that any struggling onslaught of the powers of darkness cannot touch the position of prayer.

O. CHAMBERS

When the enemy shall come in like a flood,
the Spirit of the Lord shall lift up
a standard against him.

ISAIAH 59:19

September 8

The essential meaning of prayer is that it nourishes the life of the Son of God in me and enables Him to manifest himself in my mortal flesh.

O. CHAMBERS

April 25

*L*et prayer be the key of the morning
and the bolt at night.

PHILIP HENRY

Evening, and morning,
and at noon, will I pray.

PSALM 55:17

September 7

O my brethren, do not seek to find in circumstances the explanation of prayerlessness; seek it where God's Word declares it to be, in the hidden aversion of the heart to a holy God.

A. MURRAY

Incline my heart unto thy testimonies.

PSALM 119:36

April 26

To have God thus near is to enter the holy of holies—to breathe the fragrance of the heavenly air, to walk in Eden's delightful gardens. Nothing but prayer can bring God and man into this happy communion.

E. M. BOUNDS

Let us draw near with a true heart in full assurance of faith.
HEBREWS 10:22

September 6

*P*rayer is the evidence that I am spiritually concentrated on God.

O. CHAMBERS

I set my face unto the Lord God,
to seek by prayer.

DANIEL 9:3

April 27

*M*y helpless friend, your helplessness is
the most powerful plea which rises up to the
tender father-heart of God. You think that
everything is closed to you because you
cannot pray. My friend, your helplessness
is the very essence of prayer.

O. HALLESBY

The Spirit also helpeth in our infirmities.
ROMANS 8:26

September 5

*D*etermine not to let Him go
until the blessing comes.

E. M. BOUNDS

I will not let thee go, except thou bless me.
GENESIS 32:26

April 28

*I*t is because our Lord Jesus Christ went through the depths of agony to the last ebb in the Garden of Gethsemane, because He went through Calvary, that we have "boldness to enter into the holy place."

O. CHAMBERS

Being in anguish, he prayed more earnestly.

LUKE 22:44 NIV

September 4

*I*t is the work of the Spirit to convict of sin. The quiet hour of prayer is one of the most favorable opportunities He has in which to speak to us seriously. In quietude and solitude before the face of God our souls can hear better than at any other time.

O. HALLESBY

When he giveth quietness,
who then can make trouble?

JOB 34:29

April 29

*P*rayer honors God, acknowledges His being, exalts His power, adores His providence, secures His aid.

E. M. BOUNDS

Make thy prayer unto him,
and he shall hear thee.

JOB 22:27

September 3

*n*owhere can we get to know the holiness of God and come under its influence and power, except in the inner chamber. It has been well said: "No man can expect to make progress in holiness who is not often and long alone with God."

A. MURRAY

April 30

*n*o matter what we pray for, whether it be temporal or spiritual things, little things or great things, gifts for ourselves or for others, our prayers should really resolve themselves into a quiet waiting for the Lord in order to hear what it is that the Spirit desires to have us pray for at that particular time.

O. HALLESBY

My soul waiteth for the Lord.
PSALM 130:6

September 2

When you magnify an object, you enlarge it so that you can understand it. When we magnify God, we do the same. We enlarge our awareness of Him so we can understand Him more. This is exactly what happens in the chapel of worship— we take our mind off ourselves and set it on God. The emphasis is on Him.

MAX LUCADO

May 1

After a hard day scrambling to find your way around in the world, it's assuring to come home to a place you know. God can be equally familiar to you. With time you can learn where to go for nourishment, where to hide for protection, where to turn for guidance. Just as your earthly house is a place of refuge, so God's house is a place of peace.

MAX LUCADO

September 1

*Y*ou are born into this world and will probably never know to whose prayers your life is the answer.

O. CHAMBERS

May 2

Our prayers are heard, not because we are in earnest, not because we suffer, but because Jesus suffered.

O. CHAMBERS

Christ is not entered into the holy places made with hands...but into heaven itself, now to appear in the presence of God for us.

HEBREWS 9:24

August 31

)f the whole, or the greater number of the disciples of Christianity were with an earnest and unalterable resolution of each to agree that heaven should not withhold one single influence which the very utmost effort of conspiring and persevering supplication would obtain, it would be a sign that a revolution of the world was at hand.

E. M. BOUNDS

May 3

The Holy Spirit is "the Spirit of prayer." "Ye have received the Spirit of adoption, whereby we cry, Abba, Father." The Holy Spirit is given for the express purpose of teaching us, from the very beginning of our Christian life onward, to utter that word in childlike trust and surrender.

A. MURRAY

August 30

The secret prayer chamber is a bloody battle ground. Here violent and decisive battles are fought out. Here the fate of souls for time and eternity is determined, in quietude and solitude, without another soul as spectator or listener.

O. HALLESBY

He prayed...and his sweat was as it were great drops of blood falling down to the ground.
LUKE 22:44

May 4

The real purpose of our wrestling in prayer is to render us so impotent and helpless, not only in connection with our physical and spiritual needs, but, above all, our inability to pray, that our prayer really becomes a prayer for the Spirit of prayer.

O. HALLESBY

Neither know we what to do:
but our eyes are upon thee.
2 CHRONICLES 20:12

August 29

The connection between the prayer life and the Spirit life is close and indissoluble. It is not merely that we can receive the Spirit through prayer, but the Spirit life requires, as an indispensable thing, a continuous prayer life. I can be led continually by the Spirit only as I continually give myself to prayer.

A. MURRAY

If we live in the Spirit,
let us also walk in the Spirit.
GALATIANS 5:25

May 5

*D*o you expect to go to heaven?" asked someone of a devout Scotsman. "Why, man, I live there," was the quaint and unexpected reply. It was a pithy statement of a great truth, for all the way to heaven is heaven begun to the Christian who walks near enough to God to hear the secrets He has to impart.

E. M. BOUNDS

August 28

Our lives are the answers not only to the prayers of other people, but to the prayer the Holy Spirit is making for us, and to the prayer of our Lord himself.

O. CHAMBERS

I pray for...them which thou hast given me.

JOHN 17:9

M a y   6

*P*rayer is the way the life of God is nourished. Our Lord nourished the life of God in Him by prayer; He was continually in contact with His Father.

O. CHAMBERS

August 27

The shower of answers to your prayers will continue to your dying hour. Nor will it cease then. When you pass out from beneath the shower, your dear ones will step into it. Every prayer and every sigh which you have uttered for them and their future welfare will, in God's time, descend upon them as a gentle rain of answers to prayer.

O. HALLESBY

May 7

Prayer does not mean simply to pour out
one's heart. It means rather to find the way to
God and to speak with Him, whether the
heart is full or empty. No man can do that by
himself. For that he needs Jesus Christ.

D. BONHOEFFER

*Let us therefore come boldly unto
the throne of grace.*

HEBREWS 4:16

August 26

The possibilities of prayer run parallel with the promises of God. Prayer opens an outlet for the promises, removes the hindrances in the way of their execution, puts them into working order, and secures their precious ends.

E. M. BOUNDS

May 8

I think Christians fail so often to get answers to their prayers because they do not wait long enough on God. They just drop down and say a few words, and then jump up and forget it and expect God to answer them. Such praying always reminds me of the small boy ringing his neighbor's doorbell, and then running away as fast as he can go.

E. M. BOUNDS

August 25

*N*othing but the knowledge of God, as the Holy One, will make us holy. And how are we to obtain that knowledge of God, except in...our private place of prayer? It is a thing utterly impossible unless we take time and allow the holiness of God to shine on us.

A. MURRAY

If thou seekest...then shalt thou understand the fear of the Lord, and find the knowledge of God.

PROVERBS 2:4–5

May 9

*I*n the quiet and holy hour of prayer we should be still and permit ourselves to be examined by the Physician of our souls. We should submit to scrutiny under the holy and penetrating light of God and be thoroughly examined.

O. HALLESBY

Search me, O God…
and know my thoughts.

PSALM 139:23

August 24

Avoid every tendency away from the simplicity of relationship to God in Christ Jesus, and then prayer will be as the breath of the lungs in a healthy body.

O. CHAMBERS

Let every thing that hath breath praise the Lord.

PSALM 150:6

May 10

*T*he more you know the less intelligently you pray because you forget to believe that God can alter the difficulties.

O. CHAMBERS

August 23

It is the praying heart that sanctifies the toil and skill of the hands, and the toil and wisdom of the head. Prayer keeps work in the line of God's will, and keeps thought in the line of God's Word.

E. M. BOUNDS

Bringing into captivity every thought
to the obedience of Christ.

2 CORINTHIANS 10:5

May 11

My prayer life must be brought entirely under the control of Christ and His love. Then, for the first time, will prayer become what it really is, the natural and joyous breathing of the spiritual life, by which the heavenly atmosphere is inhaled and then exhaled in prayer.

A. MURRAY

The love of Christ constraineth us.

2 CORINTHIANS 5:14

August 22

*P*ray a little each day in a childlike way for the Spirit of prayer. If you feel that you know, as yet, very little concerning the deep things of prayer and what prayer really is, then pray for the Spirit of prayer. There is nothing He would rather do than unveil to you the grace of prayer.

O. HALLESBY

May 12

*G*od has voluntarily made himself dependent also upon our prayer. For prayer is the deciding factor in the life of every one who surrenders himself to God to be used by Him.

O. HALLESBY

August 21

We learn by prayer to detect the difference between God's order and God's permissive will. God's order is—no pain, no sickness, no devil, no war, no sin: His permissive will is all these things, the "soup" we are in just now. What a man needs to do is to get hold of God's order in the kingdom on the inside, and then he will begin to see how to handle the riddle of the universe on the outside.

O. CHAMBERS

May 13

*N*o cloud obscured the face of the Father from His trusting child, who could look up into the Divine countenance and pour out the longings of his heart.

E. M. BOUNDS

Give ear to my prayer, O God; and hide not thyself from my supplication.

PSALM 55:1

August 20

*G*od's silences are His answers. If we only take as answers those that are visible to our senses, we are in a very elementary condition of grace.

O. CHAMBERS

Be still, and know that I am God.

PSALM 46:10

May 14

*G*et a place for prayer where no one imagines that that is what you are doing, shut the door and talk to God in secret.

O. CHAMBERS

He was praying in a certain place.

LUKE 11:1

August 19

Do not forget that prayer is ordained for the purpose of glorifying the name of God. Therefore, whether you pray for big things or for little things, say to God, "If it will glorify Thy name, then grant my prayer and help me."

O. HALLESBY

May 15

*P*rayer is an all-efficient panoply, a treasure undiminished, a mine which is never exhausted, a sky unobscured by clouds, a heaven unruffled by the storm. It is the root, the fountain, the mother of a thousand blessings.

CHRYSOSTOM

August 18

*P*rayer, like faith, obtains promises, enlarges their operation, and adds to the measure of their results.

E. M. BOUNDS

Unto him that is able to do exceeding abundantly above all that we ask or think.

EPHESIANS 3:20

May 16

*I*n prayer, the heart leaps to meet with God just as a child runs to his mother's arms, ever sure that with her is the sympathy that meets every need.

E. M. BOUNDS

We cry, "Abba, Father."
ROMANS 8:15 NIV

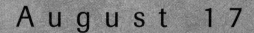

August 17

*L*et us thank God heartily as often as we pray that we have His Spirit in us to teach us to pray. Thanksgiving will draw our hearts out to God and keep us engaged with Him; it will take our attention from ourselves and give the Spirit room in our hearts.

A. MURRAY

Let us come before his presence with thanksgiving.

PSALM 95:2

May 17

We receive a great deal from God without asking for it. Simply because God is love. And the essence of love is to give: give all it has to give, give all it can give without bringing harm to the loved one, give all it can persuade the loved one to accept.

O. HALLESBY

My beloved is mine, and I am his.
SONG OF SOLOMON 2:16

August 16

Our understanding of God is the answer to prayer; getting things from God is God's indulgence of us. When God stops giving us things, He brings us into the place where we can begin to understand Him.

O. CHAMBERS

O the depth of the riches both of the wisdom and knowledge of God!

ROMANS 11:33

May 18

Watch your motive before God; have no other motive in prayer than to know Him.

O. CHAMBERS

I count all things but loss for the excellency of the knowledge of Christ Jesus my Lord.

PHILIPPIANS 3:8

August 15

*T*he Church that makes little of prayer cannot maintain vital piety and is powerless to advance the Gospel. The Gospel cannot live, fight, conquer without prayer—prayer unceasing, instant, and ardent.

E. M. BOUNDS

Pray one for another.
JAMES 5:16

May 19

*P*rayer can do anything that God can do.

E. M. BOUNDS

With God all things are possible.

MATTHEW 19:26

August 14

*P*rayer should be the means by which I, at all times, receive all that I need, and, for this reason, be my daily refuge, my daily consolation, my daily joy, my source of rich and inexhaustible joy in life.

O. HALLESBY

Cast thy burden upon the Lord,
and he shall sustain thee.

PSALM 55:22

May 20

*P*rayer brings a good spirit in our homes. For God hears prayer. Heaven itself would come down to our homes. And even though we who constitute the home all have our imperfections and our failings, our home would, through God's answer to prayer, become a little paradise.

O. HALLESBY

August 13

*S*urely the experience of all good men confirms the proposition that without due measure of private devotions the soul will grow lean.

W. WILBERFORCE

Early will I seek thee.
PSALM 63:1

May 21

Our whole prayer relationship to the Lord Jesus must be a new thing. I must believe in His infinite love, which really longs to have communion with me every moment and to keep me in the enjoyment of His fellowship.... I must believe in Him who, as the great Intercessor, through the Spirit, will inspire each member of His Body with joy and power for communion with God in prayer.

A. MURRAY

August 12

When we pray "in the Name of Jesus," the answers are in accordance with His nature, and if we think our prayers are unanswered, it is because we are not interpreting the answer along this line.

O. CHAMBERS

If ye shall ask any thing in my name, I will do it.

JOHN 14:14

May 22

Specific times and places and communion with God go together. It is by no haphazard chance that in every age men have risen early to pray. The first thing that marks decline in spiritual life is our relationship to the early morning.

O. CHAMBERS

I myself will awake early.

PSALM 57:8

August 11

Prayer is a fine, delicate instrument. To use it right is a great art, a holy art. There is perhaps no greater art than the art of prayer. Yet, the least gifted, the uneducated, and the poor can cultivate the holy art of prayer.

O. HALLESBY

May 23

There is no arriving at a high state of grace without much praying, and no staying in those high altitudes without great praying.

E. M. BOUNDS

Who shall ascend into the hill of the Lord? or who shall stand in his holy place? He that hath clean hands, and a pure heart.

PSALM 24:3-4

August 10

We are obliged to pray if we be citizens of God's Kingdom. Prayerlessness is expatriation, or worse, from God's Kingdom. It is outlawry, a high crime, a constitutional breach. The Christian who relegates prayer to a subordinate place in his life soon loses whatever spiritual zeal he may have once possessed.

E. M. BOUNDS

I will therefore that men pray every where, lifting up holy hands.

1 TIMOTHY 2:8

May 24

The goal of prayer is the ear of God. The living child of God never offers a prayer which pleases himself; he wonders that God listens to him, and he accounts it a wonderful instance of condescending mercy that such poor prayers as his should ever reach the ears of the Lord God of Sabaoth.

C. H. Spurgeon

Neither his ear heavy, that it cannot hear.
ISAIAH 59:1

August 9

*I*n the conflict between the believer and the powers of darkness, the inner chamber is the place where the decisive victory is obtained.

A. MURRAY

This is the victory that overcometh the world, even our faith.

1 JOHN 5:4

May 25

We should say to God as we mingle with our dear ones each day, "God, give them each Thy blessing. They need it, because they live with me, and I am very selfish and unwilling to sacrifice very much for them, although I do love them."

O. HALLESBY

August 8

It is impossible to live the life of a disciple without definite times of secret prayer. You will find that the place to enter in is in your business, as you walk along the streets, in the ordinary ways of life, when no one dreams you are praying, and the reward comes openly, a revival here, a blessing there.

O. CHAMBERS

May 26

A prayer offered by the humblest and most obscure saint on the ground of the Redemption of Jesus Christ demands the complete attention of God and the performance of His program.

O. CHAMBERS

August 7

Our praying, to be strong, must be buttressed by holy living. The life of faith perfects the prayer of faith.

E. M. BOUNDS

Present your bodies a living sacrifice, holy, acceptable unto God.

ROMANS 12:1

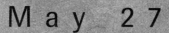

May 27

Oh, if we would only take time for the inner chamber so that we might experience in full reality the presence of this Almighty Jesus! What a blessedness would be ours through faith! An unbroken fellowship with an Omnipotent and Almighty Lord.

A. MURRAY

Holy, holy, holy, is the Lord of hosts: the whole earth is full of his glory.
ISAIAH 6:3

August 6

It is not necessary to maintain a conversation when we are in the presence of God. We can come into His presence and rest our weary souls in quiet contemplation of Him. Our groanings, which cannot be uttered, rise to Him and tell Him better than words how dependent we are upon Him.

O. HALLESBY

May 28

As we go in and out among our dear ones
day by day, we should transmit to them by
intercessory prayer that supernatural power
which will enable them to lead victorious
lives and which will put thanksgiving and joy
into their hearts and upon their lips.

O. HALLESBY

August 5

*I*f anyone wishes to do God's work, he must take time for fellowship with Him, to receive His wisdom and power. The dependence and helplessness, of which this is an evidence, open the way and give God the opportunity of revealing His power.

A. MURRAY

My strength is made perfect in weakness.
2 CORINTHIANS 12:9

May 29

Prayer is a trade to be learned. We must be apprentices and serve our time at it. Painstaking care, much thought, practice, and labor are required to be a skillful tradesman in praying. Practice in this, as well as in all other trades, makes perfect.

E. M. BOUNDS

August 4

*P*rayer is not only asking, it is an attitude of heart that produces an atmosphere in which asking is perfectly natural, and Jesus says, "every one that asketh receiveth."

O. CHAMBERS

May 30

The whole idea of the prayers of the saints is that God's holiness, God's purpose, and God's wise ways may be brought about irrespective of who comes or goes.

O. CHAMBERS

So are my ways higher than your ways.

ISAIAH 55:9

August 3

*I*t is necessary for us to withdraw at regular intervals and enable our souls to attain that quietude and inward composure which are essential if we would hear the voice of God.

O. HALLESBY

Cast me not away form thy presence.

PSALM 51:11

May 31

*I*t is true that the mightiest successes that come to God's cause are created and carried on by prayer. God's day of power; the angelic days of activity and power are when God's Church comes into its mightiest inheritance of mightiest faith and mightiest prayer.

E. M. BOUNDS

August 2

When you say, "Thy kingdom come," you are inviting the Messiah himself to walk into your world. "Come, my King! Take your throne in our land. Be present in my heart. Be present in my office. Come into my marriage. Be Lord of my family, my fears, and my doubts." This is no feeble request; it's a bold appeal for God to occupy every corner of your life.

MAX LUCADO

June 1

Come and sit and ask Him whatever is on your heart. No question is too small, no riddle too simple. He has all the time in the world. Come and seek the will of God.

MAX LUCADO

August 1

*M*en would pray better if they lived better.
They would get more from God if they lived
more obedient and well-pleasing to God.

E. M. BOUNDS

*And whatsoever we ask, we receive of him,
because we keep his commandments, and do
those things that are pleasing in his sight.*

1 JOHN 3:22

June 2

To pray is to open our hearts to Jesus. And Jesus is all that we sinners need both for time and eternity.

O. HALLESBY

He is able also to save them to the uttermost that come unto God by him, seeing he ever liveth to make intercession for them.

HEBREWS 7:25

July 31

The purpose of prayer is to reveal the presence of God equally present all the time in every condition.

O. CHAMBERS

Let us come before his presence.

PSALM 95:2

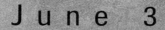

June 3

*P*rayer is not meant to develop us naturally, it is meant to give the life of the Son of God in us a chance to develop, that the natural order may be transfigured into the spiritual.

O. CHAMBERS

July 30

*F*asting helps to give us that inner sense of spiritual penetration by means of which we can discern clearly that for which the Spirit of prayer would have us pray in exceptionally difficult circumstances.

O. HALLESBY

June 4

*T*emptations which accompany the working day will be conquered on the basis of the morning breakthrough to God. Decisions, demanded by work, become easier and simpler where they are made not in the fear of men but only in the sight of God. He wants to give us today the power which we need for our work.

D. BONHOEFFER

He kneeled upon his knees three times a day.
DANIEL 6:10

July 29

The simplicity of prayer, its childlike elements form a great obstacle to true praying. Intellect gets in the way of the heart. The child spirit only is the spirit of prayer.

E. M. BOUNDS

Suffer little children...to come unto me: for of such is the kingdom of heaven.

MATTHEW 19:14

June 5

To say prayers in a decent, delicate way is not heavy work. But to pray really, to pray till hell feels the ponderous stroke, to pray till the iron gates of difficulty are opened, till the mountains of obstacles are removed, till the mists are exhaled and the clouds are lifted, and the sunshine of a cloudless day brightens—this is hard work, but it is God's work and man's best labor.

E. M. BOUNDS

July 28

*I*n the conflict between Satan and the believer, God's child can conquer everything by prayer. Is it any wonder that Satan does his utmost to snatch that weapon from the Christian, or to hinder him in the use of it?

A. MURRAY

We are more than conquerors through him.

ROMANS 8:37

June 6

*H*elplessness becomes prayer the moment that you go to Jesus and speak candidly and confidently with Him about your needs. This is to believe.

O. HALLESBY

If our heart condemn us not,
then have we confidence toward God.

1 JOHN 3:21

July 27

We lean to our own understanding, or we bank on service and do away with prayer, and consequently by succeeding in the external we fail in the eternal, because in the eternal we succeed only by prevailing prayer.

O. CHAMBERS

Lean not unto thine own understanding.
PROVERBS 3:5

June 7

The "greater works" are done by prayer because prayer is the exercise of the essential character of the life of God in us.

O. CHAMBERS

He that believeth on me...
greater works than these shall he do.

JOHN 14:12

July 26

*M*en do not love holy praying, because they do not love holy living.

E. M. BOUNDS

Search me, O God, and know my heart: try me, and know my thoughts: and see if there be any wicked way in me.

PSALM 139:23-24

June 8

*Y*ou cannot pray; you feel that all is cold and dark: why not give yourself over into My hands? Only believe that I am ready to help you in prayer. I long greatly to shed My love abroad in your heart, so that you, in the consciousness of weakness, may confidently rely on Me to bestow the grace of prayer.

A. MURRAY

My strength is made perfect in weakness.
2 CORINTHIANS 12:9

July 25

*P*rayer is something deeper than words.
It is present in the soul before it has been
formulated in words. And it abides in the soul
after the last words of prayer have passed over
our lips.

O. HALLESBY

Unto thee, O Lord, do I lift up my soul.

PSALM 25:1

June 9

Without such stated seasons the habit of prayer can never be formed; without them there is no nourishment for the spiritual life. By means of them the soul is lifted into a new atmosphere—the atmosphere of the heavenly city, in which it is easy to open the heart to God and to speak with Him as friend speaks with friend.

E. M. BOUNDS

July 24

One night alone in prayer might make us new men, changed from poverty of soul to spiritual wealth, from trembling to triumphing.

C. H. SPURGEON

With thee all night I mean to stay,
And wrestle till the break of day.

June 10

*I*f we wish to pray with confidence and gladness, then the words of Holy Scripture will have to be the solid basis of our prayer. For here we know that Jesus Christ, the Word of God, teaches us to pray. The words which come from God become, then, the steps on which we find our way to God.

D. BONHOEFFER

Thy word was unto me the joy and rejoicing of mine heart.
JEREMIAH 15:16

July 23

$\mathcal{W}$e pray pious blather, our will is not in it, and then we say God does not answer; we never asked Him for anything. Asking means that our wills are in what we ask.

O. CHAMBERS

Ye ask, and receive not,
because ye ask amiss.

JAMES 4:3

June 11

*T*here is always a suitable place to pray, to lift up your eyes to God; there is no need to get to a place of prayer, pray wherever you are.

O. CHAMBERS

*Let us offer the sacrifice of praise
to God continually.*

HEBREWS 13:15

July 22

Listen, my friend! Your helplessness is your best prayer. It calls from your heart to the heart of God with greater effect than all your uttered pleas. He hears it from the very moment that you are seized with helplessness, and He becomes actively engaged at once in hearing and answering the prayer of your helplessness.

O. HALLESBY

The Spirit itself maketh intercession for us.

ROMANS 8:26

June 12

When God's house on earth is a house of prayer, then God's house in heaven is busy and all potent in its plans and movements, then His earthly armies are clothed with the triumphs and spoils of victory and His enemies defeated on every hand.

E. M. BOUNDS

My house shall be called the house of prayer.
MATTHEW 21:13

July 21

When we calmly reflect upon the fact that the progress of our Lord's Kingdom is dependent upon prayer, it is sad to think that we give so little time to the holy exercise. Everything depends upon prayer, and yet we neglect it not only to our own spiritual hurt, but also to the delay and injury of our Lord's cause upon earth.

E. M. BOUNDS

June 13

If God does not give you something you ask for, wait on Him. He will speak with you tenderly and sympathetically about the matter, until you yourself understand that He cannot grant your prayer.

O. HALLESBY

July 20

After all the other parts of the armor had been named, Paul adds: "With all prayer and supplication in the Spirit" (Eph. 6:18). Without prayer, the helmet of salvation, and the shield of faith, and the sword of the Spirit, which is God's Word, have no power. All depends on prayer. May God teach us to believe this and to hold fast!

A. MURRAY

June 14

What folly to think that all other blessings must come from Him, but that prayer, whereon everything else depends, must be obtained by personal effort! Thank God, I begin to comprehend the Lord Jesus is himself in the inner chamber watching over me, and holding himself responsible to teach me how to approach the Father. He only demands this— that I, with childlike confidence, wait upon Him and glorify Him.

A. MURRAY

July 19

*G*od does not exist to answer our prayers,
but by our prayers we come to discern the
mind of God.

O. CHAMBERS

Let this mind be in you,
which was also in Christ Jesus.

PHILIPPIANS 2:5

J u n e   1 5

We have to pray with our eyes on God,
not on the difficulties.

O. CHAMBERS

Our eyes are upon thee.
2 CHRONICLES 20:12

July 18

*P*rayer is the one prime, eternal condition by which the Father is pledged to put the Son in possession of the world. Christ prays through His people. Had there been importunate, universal, and continuous prayer by God's people, long ere this the earth had been possessed for Christ.

E. M. BOUNDS

June 16

*I*t is hard to wait and press and pray, and hear no voice, but stay till God answers.

E. M. BOUNDS

I waited patiently for the Lord; and he inclined unto me, and heard my cry.

PSALM 40:1

July 17

There would be no hope for you if you were to pray in your own name. But listen! You are to pray in the name of Jesus. It is for Jesus' sake that you are to receive what you ask for.

O. HALLESBY

Whatsoever ye shall ask in my name, that I will do, that the Father may be glorified in the Son.

JOHN 14:13

June 17

*I*f there be anything I do, if there be anything I leave undone, let me be perfect in prayer. After all, whatever God may appoint, prayer is the great thing. Oh that I may be a man of prayer!

H. MARTYN

Watch and pray.

MARK 13:33

July 16

*B*ear up the hands that hang down, by faith and prayer; support the tottering knees. Have you any days of fasting and prayer? Storm the throne of grace and persevere therein, and mercy will come down.

J. WESLEY

Aaron and Hur stayed up his hands…
and his hands were steady until the
going down of the sun.
EXODUS 17:12

June 18

*M*y praying friend, continue to make known your desires to God in all things. It is when we can speak with one another about anything and everything that conversation really affords us freedom and relief. Let Him decide whether you are to receive what you ask for or not.

O. HALLESBY

Let your requests be made known unto God.

PHILIPPIANS 4:6

July 15

The prayer of the feeblest saint on earth who lives in the Spirit and keeps right with God is a terror to Satan. The very powers of darkness are paralyzed by prayer. No wonder Satan tries to keep our minds fussy in active work till we cannot think in prayer.

O. CHAMBERS

I will build my church; and the gates of hell shall not prevail against it.
MATTHEW 16:18

June 19

*I*f God sees that my spiritual life will be furthered by giving me the things for which I ask, then He will give them, but that is not the end of prayer. The end of prayer is that I come to know God himself.

O. CHAMBERS

Hereby we do know that we know him.
1 JOHN 2:3

July 14

*P*ray for whatsoever you will. In the name Jesus you have permission, not only to stand in the presence of God, but also to pray for everything you need.

O. HALLESBY

The Father will give you
whatever you ask in my name.

JOHN 15:16 NIV

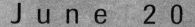

June 20

) had not understood that He was with me every day in the inner chamber, in His great love ready to keep and bless me, however sinful and guilty I felt myself to be. I had not supposed that just as He will give all other grace in answer to prayer, so, above all and before all, He will bestow the grace of a praying heart.

A. MURRAY

It is good for me to draw near to God.

PSALM 73:28

July 13

Do not strive in your own strength; cast yourself at the feet of the Lord Jesus, and wait upon Him in the sure confidence that He is with you, and works in you. Strive in prayer; let faith fill your heart—so will you be strong in the Lord, and in the power of His might.

A. MURRAY

When I am weak, then am I strong.
2 CORINTHIANS 12:10

June 21

*P*rayer should be free, spontaneous, vital fellowship between the created person and the personal Creator, in which Life should touch life. The more that prayer becomes the untrammeled, free, and natural expression of the desires of our hearts, the more real it becomes.

O. HALLESBY

The prayer of the upright is his delight.

PROVERBS 15:8

July 12

The possibilities of prayer are found in its allying itself with the purposes of God, for God's purposes and man's praying are the combination of all potent and omnipotent forces.

E. M. BOUNDS

I delight to do thy will, O my God.

PSALM 40:8

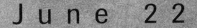

June 22

A revival of real praying would produce a spiritual revolution.

E. M. BOUNDS

Ye shall seek me, and find me, when ye shall search for me with all your heart.

JEREMIAH 29:13

July 11

The illustrations of prayer our Lord uses are on the line of importunity, a steady, persistent, uninterrupted habit of prayer.

O. CHAMBERS

Pray without ceasing.

1 THESSALONIANS 5:17

June 23

One great effect of prayer is that it enables the soul to command the body. By obedience I make my body submissive to my soul, but prayer puts my soul in command of my body.

O. CHAMBERS

That the life also of Jesus might be made manifest in our mortal flesh.

2 CORINTHIANS 4:11

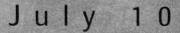

July 10

*M*ore things are wrought by prayer than this world dreams of.

TENNYSON

The effectual fervent prayer of a righteous man availeth much.

JAMES 5:16

June 24

*G*od is a rich and bountiful Father, and He does not forget His children, nor withhold from them anything which it would be to their advantage to receive.

J. K. MACLEAN

No good thing will he withhold from them that walk uprightly.

PSALM 84:11

July 9

*E*very believer who has lived with God for some time has had a number of blessed experiences in his prayer life, hours when God, so to speak, lifted him up into His lap and drew him unto His own heart, hours when He whispered into his wondering soul words which cannot be uttered.

O. HALLESBY

June 25

Why grow we weary when asked to watch with our Lord? Up, sluggish heart, Jesus calls thee! Rise and go forth to meet the Heavenly Friend in the place where He manifests himself.

E. M. BOUNDS

Could ye not watch with me one hour?

MATTHEW 26:40

July 8

*W*hen prayer fails, the world prevails.

E. M. BOUNDS

Watch and pray,
that ye enter not into temptation.

MATTHEW 26:41

June 26

)f we desire to retain our zeal for those for whom we are praying, and if their needs and distress are to move us to intercede for them daily, we will find that this does not take place without striving and wrestling on our part.

O. HALLESBY

July 7

)f your crowd knows you as a man or woman of prayer, they have a right to expect from you a nobler type of conduct than from others.

O. CHAMBERS

He heareth the prayer of the righteous.

PROVERBS 15:29

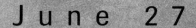

June 27

*T*ell God what you know He knows in order that you may get to know it as He does.

O. CHAMBERS

Your Father knoweth what things ye have need of, before ye ask him.

MATTHEW 6:8

July 6

*T*he soul who prays, who listens and gives heed to the Spirit's prompting concerning prayer, will experience what a joy prayer is when he prays in harmony with the Spirit of prayer.

O. HALLESBY

June 28

*B*ow before Me as one who expects everything from his Savior. Let your soul keep silence before Me, however sad you feel your state to be. Be assured of this—I will teach you how to pray.

A. MURRAY

Lord, teach us to pray.

LUKE 11:1

July 5

*G*o to your inner chamber, however cold and dark your heart may be. Do not try in your own might to force yourself into the right attitude. Bow before Him, and tell Him that He sees in what a sad state you are and that your only hope is in Him. Trust Him with a childlike trust to have mercy upon you, and wait upon Him. In such a trust you are in a right relationship to Him.

A. MURRAY

June 29

*E*very time Jesus sees that there is a possibility of giving us more than we know how to ask, He does so. And in order to do so He often has to deal with us in ways which are past our finding out.

O. HALLESBY

How unsearchable are his judgments,
and his ways past finding out!

ROMANS 11:33

July 4

*F*aith is only omnipotent when on its knees and its outstretched hands take hold of God, then it draws to the utmost of God's capacity; for only a praying faith can get God's "all things whatsoever."

E. M. BOUNDS

All things, whatsoever ye shall ask in prayer, believing, ye shall receive.

MATTHEW 21:22

June 30

There are, and there ought to be, stated seasons of communion with God when, everything else shut out, we come into His presence to talk to Him and to let Him speak to us; and out of such seasons springs that beautiful habit of prayer that weaves a golden bond between earth and heaven.

E. M. BOUNDS

July 3

*Y*our prayers move God to change the world. You may not understand the mystery of prayer. You don't need to. But this much is clear: Actions in heaven begin when someone prays on earth. What an amazing thought!

MAX LUCADO

July 1

$\int$ee that you do not use the trick of prayer
to cover up what you know you ought to do.

O. CHAMBERS

To him that knoweth to do good,
and doeth it not, to him it is sin.

JAMES 4:17

July 2